Wacked

Dave Hammer

Hey, Wanna Squeeze My Cheese?

A Book of Humor

ISBN: 978-1-4866-0548-4

Word Alive Press
131 Cordite Road, Winnipeg, MB R3W 1S1
www.wordalivepress.ca

WORD ALIVE
—P R E S S—

Cataloguing in Publication may be obtained through Library and Archives Canada

Acknowledgements

I'd like to thank everyone who's read my funny thoughts over the past few years. Hearing you laugh out loud really kept me writing humor.

A special thanks to my mom, my brother Evan, and my good friends Ken Gunn and Leta Miciak for their thoughts on making my humor writings better. To my sister Shauna, who lent her talents to drawing the illustrations inside this book, I will always be appreciative.

Introduction

In the world we live in, we could all use a good laugh, and I hope this book does just that for you. I began getting silly songs and thoughts in my head in my teens, but I only began writing them down in 2005.

I have compiled one hundred of them from the past few years. I find that the ones that don't make me laugh right away can make me laugh when I read them days, weeks, or months later. I hope you find this true for yourself. I recommend reading no more than one per day for optimal effect.

Reference to family members are *not* references to myself or other members of my family.

Dave Hammer

August 26, 2009

Grandma was a miner
She wore her boots proud
When she got to singing
She really wooed the crowd

Grandma was a brawler
She liked her coffee strong
When she got to fighting
It was best to run along

Larry was a loafer
He sat on his duff all day
He rarely did a thing
Unless he had something to say

They always wanted him to play
But he liked to spend his whole day
On his recliner chair throne
Calling for someone to bring him the phone

He lay in his chair
And moaned like a cow
He always wanted something
And he wanted it now

(To the tune of "Three Blind Mice")

Three dead mice
Boy, do they smell
They all smell like the butcher's wife
Who hasn't bathed in a fortnight
Have you ever smelled such a stench in your life
As three dead mice?

4.

The pig in a blanket
Surfed on the swells
But didn't really care
For the awful smells

It smelled like the fish
Died in their sleep
And a skunk had sprayed
All the creatures of the deep

The in-laws are coming
And bringing their kids
And also their stinky
Little dog named Figs

The poor dog
Has buckteeth
So when he grins
He looks like a hog

The two kids pick their ears
Amongst their parents' vibrant cheers
And you wonder why
We shed so many crocodile tears!

Well, slap me silly
And shoot the horse
My best friend
Was born on a course

Where the cars drive fast
In the smokin' heat
He was born
In the back seat

The baby was delivered
Doing two hundred and three
As his daddy passed the line
And won the Grand Prix

When he was young
He cleaned his ears
When there was no water
He used his tears

He whistled while he scrubbed
And he used lots of soap
Though there was no water
There was plenty of hope

As happy as could be
He shined up his toes
And when he was done
He buffed up his nose

Bill was a barber
Born under a bridge
No one ever told him
He'd never be rich

So he made a fortune
Not knowing the lie
That it shouldn't happen
To him or to I

Spring has sprung
The grass has died
Wonder why his brain is fried

He baked a cake
And sewed a dress
Wonder why his mind's a mess

He ate a cow
A big ol' steer
Wonder why his body's weird

10.

Larry's Lunchtime Rules

No Lying
No Crying
No Laughing
No Leaping
No Burping
No Slurping
No Flirting
No Sitting
No Knitting
No Gazing
No Gaping
No Sneaking
No Beating
No Fighting
No Biting
No Running
No Begging
No Bootlegging
No Loitering
No Cuffing
No Chasing

No Chewing
No Cutting
No Eating
No Lunging
No Egging
No Limping
No Leering
No Leaning
No Badgering
No Clapping

And most important of all...
No snacking

There was a greasy monkey
He pushed his hand too far
He stuck it down Ed's pant leg
To try and grab a jar

Ed squeezed his little throat
And stuck him in a tree
Now when Ed wants a banana
He fetches one for he

Then one day the monkey
Kissed Ed with a grin
It gave Ed the creeps
He yanked the hair from his chin

12.

Penny Lee
Had a bee
She stuck it in her ear

She pulled it out
Left a welt
Cinched her belt

Her tear ducts opened up
Her ear swelled shut
The doctors drilled a hole

They grinned like goofballs
When they looked inside
And yelled, "Alright!"
They'd struck oil
After all their toil

13.

He is a purple gerbil
And he lives down by the sea
He scrubs his dirty whiskers
Just to see them clean

He twitches his hairy nose
To see what he can find
Maybe he'll get into trouble
Cause he's a gerbil
Half out of his mind

Robert Platt was kinda fat
His wife was kinda lean
Together they raised a lot of kids
And none of them were mean

The kids ate lots of barley and corn
They dined on crickets and frogs
Sure drank a lot of creek water
And waved to their neighbor's dogs

They were hillbillies by nature
And their smile lacked some teeth
But they were always grinning
And runnin' to be beat

Their breath smelled like barley
Their sweat smelled like corn
They drove around in their jeep
Leaning heavily on the horn

15.

Grandma had an apple
She tried to jam it in her ear
When it wouldn't go there
She said "Oh dear…"

She was so dismayed
It put her in a slump
If she couldn't fit the apple in
How did she get so plump?

16.

Mr. Meathead the Mouse

Mr. Meathead is a mouse
A cardboard box is his house
He pounds on his homemade drum
And sits around on his bum
Mr. Meathead

He spends his days smelling dirty socks
Inside his roomy cardboard box
The smell often makes him sneeze
And then he craves stinky cheese
Mr. Meathead

Grandma had a golf club
She'd smack you in the legs
You never fooled around by her
You'd have to walk on eggs

Far down onto the green
She'd really smack her ball
Then for a bit she'd wait
But she wouldn't wait till fall

Never fool around
Not with Grandma close at hand
She'd nail you to the turf
Or bury you in the sand

"Grandma, what'd you go and do that for?"
"Quiet, boy!"

Danny hit a baseball
High into the night
When it bounced off
His neighbor's head
It gave the man a fright

The man nearly flew
Right out of his shoes
Danny ran home
Nearly peeing his pants
Hoping his neighbor
Didn't go on a rant

Larry's loose tooth
Rattled in his brain
It almost drove him nuts
He bawled from the pain

He tried to pull it out
He got a solid grip
He tried to yank it hard
But his fingers only slipped

He tied a string to his tooth
The other end to the door
Trying to get at this tooth
Was becoming quite a chore

20.

Davis was a whiner
He cried himself to sleep
When he wasn't whining
He was working on his jeep

He was such a loud whiner
He was hired to tout
Surefire cures
From desert plant burrs

It sure does cure those who whine
Cause every time they cry
You prick them with the burr
And it stops them every time!

21.

Dennis went a-running
In the grocery store
He slipped on the floor
And knocked over a family of four

As Dennis scampered off
A worker dove for his legs
But sadly he missed
And slid into the eggs

Dennis ran for the door
But the staff ran for him
So he turned right around
And went down aisle ten

He tried to make it out
But was tackled to the floor
"Can't you read the sign?" they asked
No Running In The Store

22.

Georgie was a pumpkin in the sun
Went on vacation with his mum
Never went sailing
Didn't learn to fish
Because he was a pumpkin
He married a dish

23.

Dan, he was a woodsman
He danced upon the logs
When he was much younger
He'd wrestled with the dogs

(The wild ones, that is)

He liked to play the flute all right
But if you could just hear him
You'd cover your ears with your hands
And run a screamin' into the night

The boy can't wait
To get his eyeball licked
By a dog with no brains
You're likely wondering:
What's the hurry?
Where's the gain?

25.

Way down in
The coconut tree
I found four bags
Or maybe only three
Bags of gold
And bags of gems
Back in the day
When I was only ten

26.

The sun is out
It's cookin' hot
He's frying
Lying on his cot

The birds are near
They sing their song
With his headache
It sounds like a gong

Mainly the crows
With their annoying sound
Too bad they're wild
Or he could call the pound

Thomas, he was a waiter
He dropped a lot of trays
Because of all the gigglin'
He stayed to make a name

He was known as the bungler
Who had a heart of gold

He treated everyone special
Whether young or old

Now when he drops things
And the patrons start to laugh
He's the first to join them
Then he's joined by the staff

28.

Do you want to meet K.W. Mann?
He's a mild-mannered sort
But if you ever get him offended
He'll haul you off to court!

He took me once to a ballgame
And promised before the night was out
That he'd have us both arrested
And hauled down to the old courthouse

Well, his promise didn't keep
I like to remind him of that
The evening ended, us still free
At the last swing of the baseball bat

Kenny is a farmer
He really likes to sew
While squintin' his eye
Threading the needle by the light
He even stitches up his shoe
He does a little knitting too

Even though he'd rather knit with yarn
He knows he has to clean the barn
He puts on his filthy rags
As he goes to shovel the manure into bags
Afterwards he uses a hose
But the stink makes it hard to breathe
So he tries to hold his nose

30.

The Doctor Was a Bonehead

Ted's doctor was a dunce
Tried stiffing him more than once
He could never find any wrong
Instead he sang silly songs

Then charged Ted top fee
For doing nothing, you see
The most he did was check
Reflexes in Ted's knee

Now Doc is imprisoned
He gets bread and tea
And sleeps on a mattress
Infested with fleas

31.

Jed, he was a stage man
When singing he was at his best
When he was performing
The women lost their heads
And ripped at his vest

He jumped high into the air
Then he started running
With his hat in his hand
"Let's get out of here!"
He yelled to his band.

32.

Cheesy chocolate bars
Are out of style
But they used to be the rage
For quite a while
Mothers could always tell
When their children ate them
And it wasn't by the smell
It was the chocolate and the cheese
Oozing down their chin
Pouring out their ears
And running down their knees

33.

Stinky little diapers
In a heap
Someone better clean them
Cause Tom can't sleep

Called his mom
Begged his wife
No one will do them
That's not very nice!

He called his dad
Who got quite mad
That Tom is so lazy
It's all quite sad!

Rob walked a mile to see a mule
How silly can he be?
Cause when he got there
It kicked him in the knee

The owner wouldn't sell
So Rob rested there a spell
Then he bought a dog who was brown
And rode him back to town

35.

A very Merry Christmas
And a happy New Year
I just saw your gerbil
Ride off on a reindeer

Next he'll want your Porsche
And a big fat cigar
So that he can smoke
While driving your car!

36.

Granny went golfing, all right
Only thing: she went at night
And hit the ball into the rough
Until she screamed: Enough!

The golf course was closed at night
You couldn't see a thing
You see, it wasn't lit
Not even a little bit

That didn't stop her from slicing
And driving herself mad
She sliced even in the daylight
But at least at night... no one saw her plight

37.

He thought he saw a little dog
Running down the road
But when he opened both his eyes
He saw it was a toad

I guess he should be awake
When he hits the open road
Then he wouldn't be confused
When he sees a hopping toad

38.

(To the tune of "On Top of Old Smokey")

On top of Bone Mountain
All covered with grass
I found my poor hot dog
Stuffed in the trash

It felt kind of slimy
And smelled really bad
I just shrugged my shoulders
And gave it to Dad

He cooked it up slowly
Over the heat
And then my poor hot dog
My dear dad did eat

I know that sounds awful
And in really bad taste
But Dad didn't want
That hot dog to waste

"Hey, wanna squeeze my cheese?"
Said the man in the store
Sue hit him with her purse
"Say that again
And I'll give you some more!"

He backed away quick
Fell over a stack
Got up and ran
Tripped over a rack

He fell flat on his face
Got up and fled
Right into a cart
Packed full of bread

40.

Poor Dumb Billy

The village idiot was quite the man
Sure he drank from a coffee can
But he was bright in many ways
People saw it and stopped to say

"Hey Billy, how you be?
I'm having problems with my computer, see
Would you fix it, pretty please?"

He'd fix it up as quick as could be
Cause Billy boy wasn't dumb, you see
He was quiet and shy
And a rather nice guy

41.

My chauffeur is a rat
He never cleans the floor mats
He leaves them in the car
Filthy and smelly is what they are

I fired him right there
Shoved my finger in his face
And ordered him to get!
His stinkin' carcass off my place!

Later on I hired him back
As long as he cleaned up his act
He'd have to fix the engine hose
And clip his long, hairy nose

42.

Yuckie, yuckie in a pail
Auntie got gopher guts
In the mail

Sammy is the bad boy
Who did this
When Auntie finds out
She'll have a fit

43.

Brain-dead Bob
Was a genuine slob
He drooled on his pillow
And his sheets

When he was awake
He was the friendliest sort
He'd call you up
And say, "Come over for cake!"

44.

I just bought a boat
And I sure hope it floats
Cause day after tomorrow
I'm heading out to sea

I don't want to get
Halfway to the Pole
Only to find out
The boat has a hole

45.

Mr. Dork
Has blown his cork
And now we can
All breathe again

He was like a top
All set to blow
Now that he has
He'll blow no mo'

Grandpa was a seafaring man
He didn't like the ground
He spent his time in a huge kitchen sink
Going up and down

47.

Swing your partner
Round and round
When you get tired
Just drop 'em to the ground

If you fall on top of 'em
That's all right
They won't mind
Cause you're so light

48.

Larry lost his lunch
It sailed through the air
Good thing Miss Parker ducked
Or it would have landed in her hair

He wasn't looking where he went
He tripped on the step
That's when he slipped
And on the tray lost his grip

You see, Larry was a loafer
He didn't use his head
When he was at school
He thought he was home in bed

49.

Billy kicked the bucket
He kicked it really hard
Much to his dismay
It filled his foot with shards

He went to see the doctor
Who found shards in his hair
When asked how they got there
Billy said, "Don't know, don't care
Just look at my foot
Not my hair!"

50.

Have you seen dizzy penguins?
How they do flop around
When they aren't sliding
They're moaning on the ground

They sway and tilt
Wobble to and fro
Slip on the ice
And stumble on the snow

Have you ever had your ear
Rubber-stamped, my dear?
We stamp it in the ink
And slam it on your head

It is a lot of pain
But there is plenty of gain
For one, your ear is stamped
With lots of black ink

And you've got a stain
That draws a lot of looks
To the date on your ear
Stamped just like a book

52.

In the Hayloft

In the hayloft, it's fun to play
Stick your nose down in the hay
Breathe in deep, enjoy the smell
Then go ring the dinner bell

Run across the grass real fast
Slide right through the kitchen door
Eat the pork and eat the roast
Then lie down and really snore

Put a paper on your face
It will float about in space
As you snore and sputter and blow
The paper will twirl to and fro

53.

Fred, he was a rustler
He looked just like a girl
It was mostly his hair
And all of his curls

When he wasn't rustling
He was sitting at a table
Alone he was eating some grub
Cause he was rarely in the tub

54.

Nosing for Nectar

Nosing for nectar
In the orchard trees
Peering through branches
To see what I can see
Leaping through tall grass
To where the nectar be
Slurping up nectar
Wiping my face clean

55.

Larry, Larry where ya been?
I've been downtown and back again
What ya gonna do now that you're back?
I'm gonna sit on the couch and eat a snack

56.

The dog's brain is fried
He can't find his bone
His face is hunched up like a gnome

His ears are big
His eyes are black
His jowls look like a wrinkled sack

The dog is lazy
He sleeps all day
He doesn't even like to play

When you throw
For him to fetch
All he does is yawn and stretch

57.

Frosty the snowman
Was a very lazy bum
With his sideways grin
And his small cork nose
And his brain made out of gum

He sat around
On his bum all day
And didn't have
A word to say

Yes, Frosty was
As lazy as can be
It's a good thing he melted
Early in the spring

Santa fell down the chimney
He fell right on his head
When Jimmy found him (in the morning)
He tucked the poor man in bed

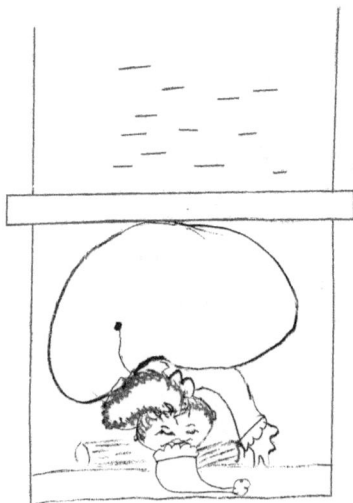

59.

(To the tune of "Six White Boomers")

Six big rednecks
Hopping mad rednecks
Chasing Santa Claus
Through the blazing sun

Seems old Santa Claus
Was a very naughty lad
He shaved their beards last night
When he crashed their pad

Now Santa's running and starting to lag
The rednecks are catching up
When they get ahold of him
They're gonna rough him up

Six big rednecks
Hopping mad rednecks
Chasing Santa Claus
Through the blazing sun

Six big rednecks
Hopping mad rednecks
On their first Christmas run

60.

The marshmallow man
Was happy as a lark
He ate lots of grubs
And plenty of bark

He was as big as a car
And as sweet as cake
When he wasn't eating
He liked to dance and shake

61.

Barley droppings
Can often be found on the floor
Just sweep them up
And send them out the door

Cover them with dirt and rot
Then put them in your cooking pot
When it comes to a boil
Add some earthy soil

When your barley soup is done
Invite your neighbors to pull up a chair
But first check the soup
And make sure you remove any hair

If they like the soup and say it's good
Don't tell them your secret
Or they might take you outside
And give you a physical ride

Drag you up and down the street
Then give you a candy sweet
Tell you that all is square
But next time, no more hair

'Tis the season
To be freezin'
Wrap yourself up
And head on out

Grab your gloves
And your shovel
The snow is deep
The driveway is steep!

When you're done
Go on in and see your hon
Get 'em to slap you hard
To get back circulation
You lost in the yard

Marcel Lebouf was a canny man
He baked a lot of pies
Put treasure maps in every one
And raised the price to the sky

He sang a lot in the shower
At the top of his high-pitched voice
Even though the maps were fake
He treated himself to lots of cake

He dried himself off with his cash
Because he had so much to spare
But paper money was not very good
For him to dry his hair

64.

Batman and Robin

"Holy cow pies, Batman!"

"What? Did I just step in one?" Batman asked, looking down where he had just stepped

"No, not that! Look up there!" Robin said.

"Where?" Batman asked, looking up at the sky, a little confused

"A bird? A plane? ...it's Superman!" Robin said.

"You're crazy! I know Superman has put on a lot of weight, but that's the Goodyear blimp!"

65.

Swahili Joe
Was stuck in the snow
Eating his toast and jam
When along came a grader
That buried him till later
As he tried to think of a plan

66.

Dipsy was a teddy bear
He lived under the stairs
Cause when he was younger
He hid there when scared

Dipsy couldn't forget the past
Because he was a dork
Wasn't really his fault
His brain was made of cork

67.

Looks like Granny is going golfing
She is dear to my heart
I'd like to be her caddy
And drive the golf cart

I'd hang with her 24/7
I love to see her smile
Just to hear her laugh
Would be well worth my while

68.

You just got grease
In my hair
Have you lost your mind?
Or just your underwear?

Your underwear
Is in the trees
It's flowing freely
In the breeze

Last year, it was up the pole
And had a lot of ragged holes
Your underwear
Is really old
At least that's what
I've always been told

Logan, Logan
Where do you live?
"I live in the freezer
So don't you dare grin!

"My cheeks are froze
My nose is cold
My clothes are covered
With many holes"

70.

Larry's lunch was on the loose
It was a scrumptious fatted goose
It ducked and twirled just out of reach
Till Larry ran screaming into the street
His stomach rumbled and gnawed away
He couldn't believe the awful pain
But he couldn't catch that dratted goose
Though he tried the entire day

HONK —

71.

If Sam were a big fat slob
He'd rob a bank in his big old Dodge
He'd drive right in
Get his bag filled up
And then he'd order a 7 Up

72.

There was a man in the country
Who liked to drive a hog
Some people might call him Larry
But to you, he's bare-chested Bob!

He likes to ride his Harley
He rides around mostly bare
Some people think he's crazy
But maybe he's just not all there

73.

Billy was a farmer
He planted lots of corn
When nothing started growing
He got a lot of scorn

So he tore down some neighbors' fences
And burned a few of their barns
Yet he was really grateful
That no one came to harm

Deep down, he was a good man
Being scorned made him mad
He wanted to strike at others
Whether they were good or bad

It was hard to fight their judgments
That's why he wrecked their place
If he had thought more clearly
He might have given them grace

74.

Diaper boy
Had a wooden toy
Jammed far up his nose
The doc was called
In the middle of fall
And found it rather funny
He pulled it out
Of the little boy's snout
And charged a lot of money

75.

Bob was a woodsman
He lived among the trees
When he wasn't working
He was busy raising bees

Then one day one stung him
Right on his eye
It swelled right shut... and strangely
Turned him off of pie

76.

Buzzard-lip Bob
Was born a slob
But he walked away from it

He made a few grand
And became a good man
And now he's better off for it

77.

In the Hospital

Jim went for a walk
In his hospital gown
Everyone he passed
Gave him a frown

The hospital gown
Showed off his rump

People were upset
Even though it was plump

He covered himself up
And ran back to bed
He was so embarrassed
Until it happened to Fred

78.

The nurse came a-running
With a needle in her hand
Pulled down Jim's pants
And jammed it right in

He let out a howl
Cause the pain was so much
And then down the hall
Came Mr. Benjamin Small

He stuck his head in
And said, "What's all the fuss?
I'm trying to watch a show
Could you keep the noise low?"

Jim nodded his head
Cause he couldn't really speak
The nurse patted his knee
And then pinched his cheek

Sneaky, Sneaky was his name
Sneaking up on you was his game
He'd find you in the loo
Surprise you at the zoo

Tap on your shoulder
Tug on your hair
Gives you a wedgie
With your underwear

He'd yank down your shorts
Mess up your hair
So if you catch him
Tie him to a chair

Call the cops
Phone your ex
If Sneaky gets loose
They'll be next

80.

Working from Home

Hotdog Tom's done!
Now he can put away his gun
And stop dreamin' of his fingers
Around his boss's throat

He's going home
To cook the goat
Cut it into strips
And shove it down his throat

He's gonna dance around
Wave his hands into the air
As he heads home to work
Until he's a millionaire!

Earl's back was in such pain
When he came through the door
He just let his body fall
And slammed to the floor

He pulled himself along the rug
Crawling towards the bed
When he finally made it there
He needed to rest his head

He dreamed of his dog Who-Knew
Who was wearing a bright red shoe
The dog just sat and laughed at him
With a funny toothless grin

82.

Cousin Larry is in town
He heard that Tim is moving
Tim just needed a change
Larry suggested he become a clown

Tim's not moving to a different town
No, just moving out of his job
Trying his hand at something else
While trying not to be a slob

He's off to make his millions
So he can help others out
Like buying a limo for his dog
Or a bicycle for his pet hog

83.

Mary was a golfer
And she was very keen
She liked to bank her shots
Off the nearby trees

Ridiculous, you say?

Well, she never got stuck
Or had a bad lie
She made all the pros
Break down and cry

84.

Commander: Well, Buzz, looks like the suit has been dropped

Buzz: Not in front of anyone I hope, sir?

Commander: Of course it was! It was in the courtroom with plenty of witnesses. Haven't you ever had a suit dropped?

Buzz: Never with witnesses, sir!

Commander: Are you trying to be funny, soldier?

85.

Poor Kid

He had to go to the bathroom
Down by the old mill stream
He went in an old outhouse
Sadly, though, it was a dream

He dreamt he went to the latrine
And then came all the way home
Later he woke up with a start
But when the smell told him this was no dream
That's when he opened his mouth and screamed

86.

Loser Larry was quite a stud
His doggie's name
Was Elmer Fudd

He dressed in jeans
He liked to strut
No one really noticed
They only watched his mutt

His mutt was rather homely
He sneezed a lot, it seems
And one day he sneezed
All over Larry's jeans

87.

He found a dead dog
In the middle of the road
He honked his horn
But it didn't move

So he got out
And screamed at it
When it didn't budge
He rolled it in the ditch

Later he told his friends
But when he described the dog
They fell off their chairs laughin'
And told him it was actually a log

88.

Jenny thought she was a pigeon
Pecking at the grain
When she flew off the balcony
She experienced a bit of pain

Luckily she was on the first floor
Since she couldn't really fly
Sure, she was kinda crazy
Cause she tried this every night

89.

Oh, the dog went down to town
Saw a piglet wearing a crown
When he made fun of it
An ant gave him a frown

Now the dog has come back
With his jaw rather slack
He whined to his owner
To give him a snack

He'd never seen a frown on an ant
Seeing such things made him pant
But he felt better after the snack
Which made his jaw less slack

*It doesn't pay to make fun of a
piglet wearing a crown*

90.

The kangaroo is eating
Jack's dad is snoring on the couch
The kangaroo is so huge
He could fit Jack's dad in his pouch

He could take the dad for a walk
And could bounce all around
While the dad's head bobbed
With each jump—up and down

91.

Pete found Grandpa's scooter
Down by the swamp
Had he been eaten by a gator?
That's not what the family would want
But they were really lucky
For Pete found him much later
Later in the day, taking a nap
Under an old willow tree
With a book on his chest
Pretending he could read

92.

Let's get to work, Kirk!
So we can make lots of money
Or follow your heart, Bart
And you'll be always happy

93.

Grandma lost her pancreas
In the middle of the sea
Then she went diving for clams
Even though she couldn't see

She didn't use her scuba gear
So bobbed back up like a giraffe
It made the dolphins clap and cheer
And do their belly laugh

94.

Jim got up early in the morning
And sat at the table to eat
He got two thick slabs of bread
Covered in lard and a diced beet

The next day, he got up
At one with a yawn
It was afternoon
And the morning was gone

But no one was there to feed him
Which really spared his tastebuds
So he had butter on two slabs of bread
And then went right back to bed

95.

Kenny Benugel was
A great big hairy man
He stuck his nose in the bacon
While it was frying in the pan

Burnt it pretty good
So he covered it with grease
Cause he wanted to ease the pain
Then he got too close to the burner
And his nose burst into flame

96.

Lorne was a lunchbox
He crept around at night
He liked to sleep in the cupboard
Out of all the light

Lorne the lunchbox got carried to school
And at night placed back by the sink
If he hadn't been cleaned for a few days
He really began to stink

97.

Well, kiss my wine-stained lips
Ignore all the drips
It is so disgusting
I know I should quit

But until tomorrow
Pucker up, honey
Or I'll look rather funny
Standing here alone
With my lips puckered up

98.

Ed hasn't bathed for an hour
He's very sorry to say
He hasn't bathed for an hour
So please get out of his way

Jim hasn't bathed for a day
Yes, it's true
So would you please
Stop saying "p u"

Ted hasn't bathed for a week
Why should you care?
Just stand back ten paces
And try not to stare

99.

Take your hand
Grab some elderberries
From a group of kids
Jam them up your nose
Until the sun shines in

100.

Extreme cures
They may be extreme, but they might just work.
Not to be tried at home

Pounding headache?
Dunk your head in a bucket of ice water

Nose running?
Cork it!
Insert two corks slowly into nostrils

Can't sleep?
Tie big rock to strong stick. Bang on head.
Repeat as needed.

About the Author

At the age of five, when most children are playing outside with friends, Dave Hammer was lying in a hospital bed, horribly burned through no fault of his own. His creativity helped him learn to do everything despite the odds against him. Now he uses his creativity to write books. His first book, From Out of the Flames: A True Story of Survival, tells the account of his life. His second book, Wacked: Hey Wanna Squeeze My Cheese?, is filled with funny poems showcasing his special brand of humor. His third book, Max Greebly and the Mystery of the Bawling Bank Robbers, is a fun adventure-mystery for younger readers. Dave is an avid reader and lives in Western Canada where he writes full-time.

www.ingramcontent.com/pod-product-compliance
Lightning Source LLC
LaVergne TN
LVHW021402080426
835508LV00020B/2404